Minerva and Arachne and the Weaving Contest

Children's Greek & Roman Myths

BABY PROFESSOR

EDUCATION KIDS

Hello kids!

What are your amazing talents?

Is weaving one of them?

Do you remain humble as you gain recognition for your talents?

In this book,
you will find
interesting
facts about
Arachne and her
connection to the
Goddess Minerva.

Who is Minerva?

Minerva was the Roman goddess of wisdom, medicine, arts, poetry and handicrafts. Later she became the goddess of war. The beautiful Minerva was also one of the virgin goddesses.

Romans believed that Minerva sprung out from the head of her father, the mighty ruler of the heavens, Jupiter. Her counterpart in Greek mythology was the goddess Athena.

She became a
favorite daughter
of Zeus. That is
one reason that
Athena became
very powerful.

Like Athena, Minerva was the goddess of crafts. She was known as the patroness of handicrafts, spinning and weaving.

Who is Arachne?

In the myth, Arachne was a skillful weaver who was very proud of what she could do. There are several versions of her story; however, all versions describe her as boastful.

She was the daughter of Idmon, a wool dyer. Arachne became famous in Lydia because of her notable weaving skills. Finally, Arachne challenged Minerva to a weaving contest.

The Story of the
Weaving Contest.

As Arachne became popular because of her weaving skills, she boasted about her skill. Even the forest nymphs appreciated Arachne's weaving skills.

Arachne told people that she was better than the goddess Minerva. She became conceited. She bragged of her awesome weaving skills.

She didn't even thank the person who taught her to weave. All this made Minerva very angry. The boastful Arachne challenged Minerva to a weaving contest.

Upon learning this, Minerva disguised herself as an old woman and went to Lydia to talk to Arachne, to try to convince her to take back the challenge.

She told Arachne
to respect the
Gods and to
take back her
challenge.
Arachne was
so furious that
she raged at the
old woman.

Then, suddenly, the old woman transformed into the beautiful Minerva. Arachne was shocked. However, she still wanted to go on with the contest.

The weaving contest went on, and Minerva won. Arachne became hopeless and depressed because of her loss.

Terribly
discouraged,
Arachne hung
herself. Athena
transformed
Arachne into
a big spider.

Visit
BABY PROFESSOR
EDUCATION KIDS
www.BabyProfessorBooks.com
to download Free Baby Professor eBooks
and view our catalog of new and exciting
Children's Books

www.ingramcontent.com/pod-product-compliance
Lightning Source LLC
Chambersburg PA
CBHW060144120726
48003CB00009B/3019